Emily and the Shackleford Horses

Written by Melissa C. Marsted
Illustrated by Izzy Greer

LUCKY PENNY
PUBLISHING

Emily and the Shackleford Horses

By Melissa C. Marsted
Illustrated by Izzy Greer

Published by:
Lucky Penny Press, a division of Lucky Penny Publishing, LLC
1776 Park Avenue
Suite 4-369
Park City, UT 84060-5148
info@luckypennypress.com

A portion of the proceeds of Emily and the Shackleford Horses will benefit
Friends of the North Carolina Maritime Museum
www.maritimefriends.org

ISBN 978-1-938136-55-9

Emily and the Shackleford Horses

Hurricane Isabel was approaching rapidly. The storm was going to be big. Really big. The rain pelted the gutters, and branches lashed against the houses of the Outer Banks, North Carolina.

"Mom, Mom, we can't leave Marilyn. Where will she and the other horses go? Who will take care of them?" cried Emily anxiously. Her mom hurried around the house gathering food and clothes to take with them as the family prepared to drive inland away from the approaching storm.

"Emily, honey, I know you're worried, but everything is going to be okay. Put your shoes on and head to the car. I'll be right there," urged Emily's mother.

Emily always worried about the horses whenever her family had to leave their home on Harkers Island because of storms, but this time was different. Marilyn, one of the Shackleford horses, was pregnant.

"Marilyn will be fine. I promise, Emily. The horses are survivors. We'll check on them as soon as we can. Right now we need to think about our own safety."

8

It was late in the season for one of the Shackleford horses to be expecting a foal. The Cape Lookout National Seashore park rangers monitored her progress, but the storm, Hurricane Isabel, was fast moving and everyone on the Outer Banks was required to move inland. Even the rangers were leaving their posts.

Stuffing the last boxes in the car, Emily's mom called, "Emily! In the car now! Hurry!"

"Mom, what about Marilyn?" cried Emily.

"She'll be fine. Really. We need to leave now."

Safely inside the car, Emily and her family traveled to their grandparents' house.

"Mom, how long will we be gone? What about Marilyn?" Emily asked.

As the family drove, they listened to the news on the radio. "Hurricane storm warnings are in place from Cape Fear southward to South Santee River in South Carolina and north from Chincoteague to New Jersey. The governors of Virginia and North Carolina have already declared states of emergency. Residents are urged to evacuate. Heavy winds are already measuring 65 miles per hour. The storm is expected to bring a storm surge of seven to 11 feet above normal ocean levels."

Hurricane Isabel hit the coast with force. Waves crashed on the shores and pulled boats from their moorings. Strong winds lashed the coast. Many residents lost electricity as uprooted trees fell on telephone lines.

Emily and her family spent five days with her grandparents. Then it was time to return home. As their car approached the neighborhood, branches and debris littered the streets for miles. Huge puddles reflected the now peaceful sky. Many of the homes were badly damaged. Her family worked together with their neighbors to clean up, mending fences and clearing broken glass, yet all Emily could think about was Marilyn and the new foal.

Another week passed. The weather had cleared. In fact, life on Harkers Island was relatively calm again. Finally, a weekend came when Emily's parents agreed to visit the Shackleford horses. Loaded with a picnic lunch and beach towels, the family took the ferry out to the landing at the Shackleford Banks close to the Cape Lookout Ranger Station. As soon as the ramp was down, Emily raced off the ferry to the station where Jake, a ranger she knew well, worked.

"How are the horses? How is Marilyn? Has she had her foal? Where is she?" she asked.

"Slow down, slow down, young lady. The horses are fine. All of them including Marilyn. And…Miss Isabel." Jake said.

"Miss Isabel?" asked Emily.

"Yes, Miss Isabel. That's what we named her. In honor of Hurricane Isabel. If you go over on that dune you'll see them, but be careful! Don't make too much noise. You don't want to scare Miss Isabel," warned Jake.

"Oh, thank you! Thank you so much!" Emily called as she raced off.

Emily ran ahead of her family to the top of the dunes where she could look out over the island. The horses loved to saunter across the dunes, roaming in search of water. They waded through the channels, digging wells with their hooves and sipping the brackish water.

Emily tumbled from dune to dune, searching for Marilyn and Miss Isabel. Finally, she spotted them together in the distance. She stopped and stared in amazement.

When her mother caught up, Emily said with tears in her eyes, "Oh Mom, I'm so happy Marilyn is okay. Isn't Miss Isabel cute?"

Her mom smiled. "Yes, Emily. Miss Isabel is absolutely adorable, just like you. I love you, Emily."

"I love you too, Mom. And our family. And Miss Isabel!"

"How about if we set up our picnic blankets and have our lunch right here. We can spend all day with Marilyn and Miss Isabel before we say goodbye until next summer."

"Thanks, Mom. This is the best day ever."

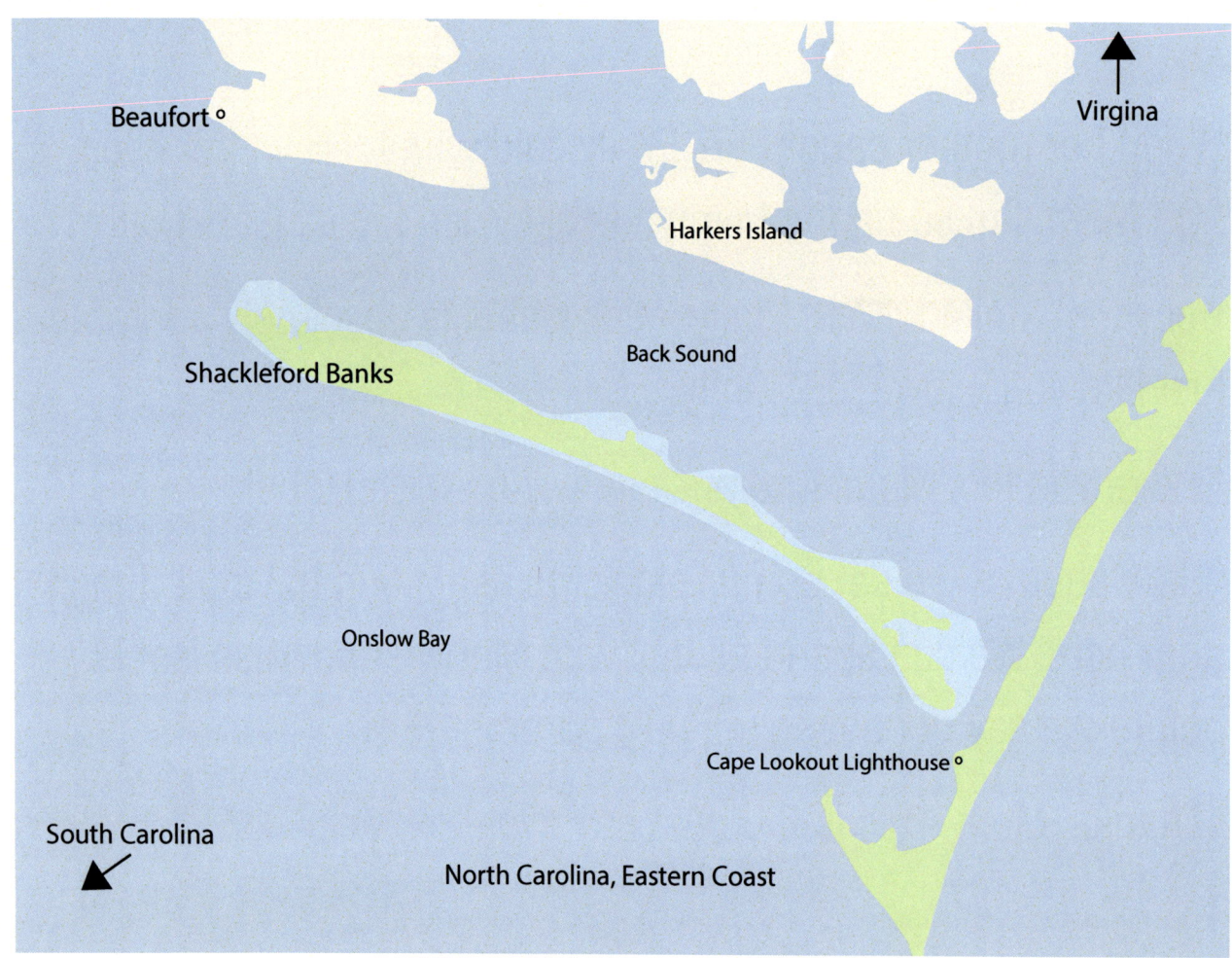

Beaufort °

Virgina

Harkers Island

Shackleford Banks

Back Sound

Onslow Bay

Cape Lookout Lighthouse °

South Carolina

North Carolina, Eastern Coast

Fun Facts
About the Shackleford Horses

The horses live on a nine-mile island called the Shackleford Banks off the coast of North Carolina in Cape Lookout National Seashore.

Between 110-130 wild horses live in about 30 groups and roam across the island's dunes. They have to search for their own food and water. They are not fed by humans.

The Shackleford Banks often face dramatic weather conditions like Hurricane Isabel in 2003. The weather can change the shape of the island and erode beaches. The horses have learned to adapt to the harsh weather conditions and protect themselves and their foals.

Legends suggest the horses are descendants of Spanish mustangs from the 1500s that may have survived shipwrecks and ended up on the island.

Visitors can either take a private boat or ferry to the island to visit the horses. Then the fun begins in search of finding where the horses might be hiding.

Both the National Park Service, Cape Lookout National Seashore and the Foundation for Shackleford Horses offer additional information about the horses.

ABOUT THE ILLUSTRATOR

Izzy Greer graduated from Williams College with degrees in Studio Art and History. Inspired by experiences of art in relation to the Tea Fire, Izzy sought to explore the relationship between art, trauma, and hope. She wrote her senior thesis, entitled "The Art of Survival," on how Holocaust survivors use art as a way to not just survive but thrive in a post-Holocaust life. She was awarded the William Bradford Turner Prize in History for her work. Now, Izzy works as a freelance graphic designer based out of San Francisco, CA.

ABOUT THE AUTHOR

Melissa C. Marsted is the Publisher and Founder of Lucky Penny Publishing, LLC as well as a long distance runner, creative writer, traveler and proud mother of two college age sons.

The idea for Lucky Penny Publishing came to Melissa after the Santa Barbara Tea Fire in November, 2008 where she lost her home of 16 years. She was working on her first children's picture book at the time and decided to invest some of the insurance proceeds into Lucky Penny Press as eBook company and launched the first eCommerce site in November, 2011. Emily and the Shackleford Horses was the second book that was illustrated for Lucky Penny Press.

She has been realizing her vision of combining all of her passions—creative writing, reading, education, art, poetry and supporting non-profits—in one complete business. With over 70 products created in the last four years for Lucky Penny Press and Silver Dollar Press, Melissa has come to believe that if you find and follow your passions then work is a dream. Melissa continues to pick up coins on her runs, trusting in the company that she has worked so hard to create. Melissa lives in Park City, Utah with her sons, William and Peter, and their Jack Russell terrier, Aro and two cats, Einstein and Midnight.

About Lucky Penny Press

Lucky Penny Press, a division of Lucky Penny Publishing, is a children's eBook
and print publishing company. Lucky Penny Press publishes books written
by both adults and children with some of our books published in multiple languages including
Spanish, French, and Chinese and with audio recordings.
All of the books advocate messages and lessons that focus on
nurturing the creative spirit, introducing new cultures, and empowering children
to believe in their dreams. Many of the themes of our books focus on
stories of adventure, nature, culture, and the environment.
As part of Lucky Penny Press's cultural fabric, each book is connected
to a non-profit organization that receives a portion of the proceeds.

A portion of the proceeds of Emily and the Shackleford Horses will benefit
Friends of the North Carolina Maritime Museum

www.maritimefriends.org

1776 Park Avenue, Suite 4-369 | Park City, UT 84060-5148 | info@luckypennypress.com

Made in the USA
San Bernardino, CA
14 June 2017